Date Due

JAN 31	JAN 14		
FEB 7	FEB 4		
Nov. 7	OCT 5		
NOV 7	FEB 8		
OCT 9			
Oct. 9			
OCT 28			
OCT 30			
MAR 5			
Mar 5			
MAR 26			
APR 8			
APR 16			
APR 25			
APR 30			
NOV 22			

NO. 340	PRINTED IN U.S.A.	BECKLEY-CARDY CO.

The Discovery Books are prepared

under the educational supervision of

Mary C. Austin, Ed.D.

Reading Specialist and

Lecturer on Education

Harvard University

A DISCOVERY BOOK

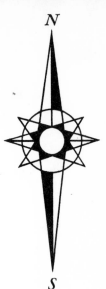

GARRARD PUBLISHING COMPANY
CHAMPAIGN, ILLINOIS

Richard E. Byrd

Adventurer to the Poles

by *Adèle deLeeuw*

illustrated by Al Fiorentino

For Tippy's friends—

Scotty and Ricky

Contents

Richard E. Byrd: Adventurer to the Poles

Chapter *1*

An Exciting Letter

The letter was sent to him, Richard Evelyn Byrd. It had a strange stamp. Richard opened it in great excitement.

He read it over three times to make sure he had not dreamed it. His father's friend, Judge Carson, was inviting him out to the Philippine Islands!

Richard knew where the Philippines were, but not many of his friends knew. They were islands far out in the Pacific Ocean. Two years ago, in 1898, the United States had won them from Spain. Judge Carson had been sent there by the United States government. He was a lawyer, like Richard's father.

When his father came home, Richard said, "I'm going to the Philippines to visit Judge Carson."

"Nonsense," his father said. His mother just smiled.

"But may I go? I'll write him tonight."

"Not so fast, young Richard," his father said. "It's a long trip for a boy of twelve to take alone. Why not stay here in Virginia a few more years?"

Richard blinked fast. His mother's eyes went from him to the pictures of his ancestors hanging on the wall. They had all been adventurers and fine, daring gentlemen. Richard was like them. There would be no stopping him.

His brothers, Tom and Harry, were interested. Richard was the middle brother. The three boys did everything together. They swam, and boxed, and made forts on the lawn. Their father had taught them to ride and shoot.

"Why do you want to go?" his brothers asked him.

"Because it's far away. It's different. I want to see new things."

It was hard to explain. He loved his family. He loved his beautiful Virginia home with its fields and tall trees.

He had a happy life, playing, hunting and fishing. Just the same, he knew the Philippines would be new and different.

It took him a long time to make his parents say he could go. At last his father gave in. His mother packed his bags. Her eyes were filled with tears. Richard stood in the doorway watching her.

After a struggle he said, "If it makes you feel sad, Mother, I won't go." He drew a big breath. His voice was quiet. "But if you don't let me go, I shall never forgive you."

His mother said gently, "Then go, Richard."

Chapter 2

Around the World Alone

Richard's mother took him to Washington. She saw him off on the train. His face was so covered with poison oak that his eyes were almost closed. His mother was crying. He didn't feel very good himself.

His spirits rose on the way to San Francisco. He kept looking at his tickets to make sure he had not lost them. He was on his own now!

Later, on the *Sumner,* the captain let him "help run the ship." At least, so Richard thought.

In the China Sea they ran into a terrible storm. Railings were smashed. Lifeboats were broken. The smokestack was carried away by the high waves.

"Go down below, Dick. Take care of that schoolteacher who feels so sick. See what you can do for her."

Richard put a cold cloth on her head. "You'll feel better soon."

She looked at him gratefully. If a young boy could be so calm, she would try to be calm too.

Richard helped all he could. The ship was four days late getting into harbor. Before the passengers left, they thanked Richard for what he had done.

The days in the Philippines were full of excitement. Some natives were hiding deep in the jungle, waiting to kill the Americans. They wanted to rule the Philippines themselves.

Soldiers were busy hunting the rebels. Sometimes Judge Carson let Richard go with them. Richard felt very proud. He had a great pistol strapped to his side.

One day they were going through the jungle. Suddenly a knife flew through the air. Shots whistled about their heads. Richard tried to draw his pistol.

A big Philippine policeman threw Richard to the ground. He would not let Richard get up until the rebels were captured. Richard marched back beside them. This time he kept his hand right on his pistol!

He wrote home of his adventures. The newspapers printed his stories. One letter told about his thirteenth birthday. A native governor gave him a party fit for a prince.

There was much sickness among the natives. Richard wanted to help the doctor. One day he took the pulse of a sick man. Later the man died of a terrible sickness called the plague.

The doctor would not let anyone leave the village. This kept the sickness from spreading. It was hard to get food. At Christmas, Richard had to eat parrot, monkey and canned plum pudding.

Judge Carson said Richard must go home. He was put on a trading ship. He traveled across the Indian Ocean, the Mediterranean and the Atlantic.

Finally he arrived in Boston. Twelve newspaper men met him. They asked him all kinds of questions. He was the youngest person of his time to travel around the world alone.

Chapter *3*

Annapolis

"Hey, Dicky-Byrd!"

"Tweet-tweet, Dicky-Byrd!"

Sixteen-year-old Richard grinned to himself. He was the youngest member of his class at Virginia Military Institute. Everyone teased him.

It was night and Richard was on guard duty. The wind sang through the tall pines. The stars and the wind made him think of those nights on the ship to the Philippines. He loved life at sea.

19

It would be fine to command a ship of his own. When he was home for vacation he told his parents.

"Good idea," his father said. "We'll see about getting you into the Academy at Annapolis." That was where young men learned to be officers in the U. S. Navy.

In two years Richard was old enough to enter Annapolis. There he studied hard. He went out for sports and made many friends.

Then trouble came. He fell in a football game. His foot was broken in three places. Would this be the end of sports for him, he wondered?

Soon there was another blow. Admiral Peary reached the North Pole. The world was thrilled, but Richard was sad.

He had wanted to go there. He had dreamed of being the first man to see the North Pole.

His dreams went back to his teens. He had written in his diary, *"Someday I'm going to explore the Pole."* Now Peary had reached it. What wonderful adventures were left in the world?

Richard's foot was better now. But when his class went to sea for naval training, he became sick with typhoid fever. He was put ashore in England and was in a hospital for two months.

When he returned to the Academy he was thin and underweight. Just the same, he went out for sports again. He was quarterback on the football team. But the games were too much for him now. He had to give them up.

He was still captain of the gym team. One day he did a dangerous stunt on the flying rings. His hand slipped. He fell thirteen feet to the floor.

His leg was broken in four places. It was the same leg he had hurt before. There were long days in the hospital again. His teachers thought he should drop back a class to catch up with his studies.

Richard Byrd said, *"I'm proud of my class. I want to graduate with it."*

And he did.

They wrote of him in the yearbook, *"Go where he may, he cannot hope to find the truth and beauty of which he dreams."*

They did not know what great adventures lay ahead of him.

Chapter *4*

Wings for a Byrd

Byrd felt proud and happy as a young ship's officer. He worked hard. But one day he fell through an opening on the ship's deck. He hurt the leg he had broken at Annapolis. Once more he was in the hospital for three months. A silver pin was put inside his leg. It was there the rest of his life.

He got out of the hospital in the spring of 1914. The First World War began in Europe that summer. Byrd limped badly. But he longed to be sent abroad. He felt sure the United States would fight.

First he was sent to Mexico. His ship stayed in a harbor there. One day a cry went up. "Man overboard! Man overboard! He'll be eaten by sharks!"

Byrd jumped into the water with all his clothes on. He swam to the drowning man. He held him up in the rough water. A line was tossed to him. He put it under the sailor's arms. He waited until the sailor was pulled up on deck. Then he let them pull him up.

Much later the government awarded Byrd the Life-Saving Medal of Honor.

That was the first his family or friends knew about his rescue of the sailor!

One day Byrd was invited to take a ride in a flying boat. That was the kind of plane that could take off and land on the water. Byrd was excited. Planes in those days were small and not at all strong. Passengers and pilot sat in the open cockpit.

Byrd loved the rush of air and the sound the motor made. It gave him a new idea. He would be a flier!

He wrote to his father about his wish. His father said, "Nonsense! You had better stay on the earth or the sea."

Soon afterwards Byrd was married to his childhood sweetheart, Marie Ames. It was a beautiful wedding. His two brothers were his two best men.

Byrd was made an officer on the President's yacht. Other young men would have been happy about this, but not Byrd. He wanted to take part in the war. Above all, he wanted to fly. But the doctors said he was too thin.

"If you let me fly," he begged the doctors, "I'll gain weight."

"Very well," they said. "We'll give you a month's trial."

A short time later Byrd stood on the white beach at Pensacola, Florida. Beyond were the buildings of the Naval Training Station. He watched a plane as it rose into the blue sky.

His heart rose with it. Soon *he* would be climbing and dipping in the bright sky. He would be a pilot with the best of them!

It was only fourteen years since the first plane had flown. There was much to learn and to do. A whole new world was opening because men had learned to fly.

Suddenly the noise of the motor stopped. The plane dropped like a fallen bird, down, down, into the sea. A fountain of water rose into the air.

Boats put out to sea. But the plane and the flier were gone. At supper the men were sad. This was but one of their friends who had lost his life.

After six hours of flying time, Byrd was ready to make his first flight alone.

"Don't stay in the air more than 20 minutes," his teacher said.

"I won't," Byrd promised. His eyes were on his plane. He longed to start.

Byrd steered the plane across the field and rose into the sky. This was his most thrilling moment. He was up in the sky, alone! Further and further he went. When he finally landed, he had been gone an hour. His teacher was angry.

"It costs a lot of money to train you people!" he shouted. "Every time a plane crashes it costs money. Don't forget that!" Then, seeing Byrd's face, he added, "You flew all right. You'll get your wings."

Byrd was sure now that he could get abroad and into the war. But the Navy wanted him to stay where he was to train other men. He had orders to teach 100 fliers to fly at night.

First he must learn to do it himself.

People had seldom flown at night before. It was too hard to see in the dark. And even in the daytime, no one flew far out to sea for fear of getting lost over the water.

Byrd had an idea. He put a compass on a plane and tried the first out-of-sight-of-land flight. He invented an instrument to show which way the wind was blowing. That would help to keep planes on their course.

Byrd was excited. Now perhaps someone could fly across the Atlantic Ocean! He longed to try it himself.

But he was ordered to Halifax, Nova Scotia, on the east coast of Canada. He was put in charge of a supply base for warships. It was a big job and he did it well.

Suddenly the war was over. Byrd was told to return home. He felt that his career was ruined. He had not been able to fight in the air or at sea. There was nothing ahead of him, he thought.

Chapter 5

Disappointment

Now Byrd began to dream of the North Pole again. In the past, men had explored on foot in the Arctic, the area farthest north. Sleds pulled by dog teams carried their supplies. Such trips were slow and difficult.

Byrd thought he could explore in a new way, by plane. He could learn more in one short trip than the other men had learned in many months.

Byrd told the Navy about his plan.

Finally, they gave him two planes. He needed more. And he needed men.

Another American explorer, Donald MacMillan, was also planning a trip to the Arctic. Byrd went to him and said, "Why don't we go together? You have one plane from the Navy, and I have two."

MacMillan wanted to lead the trip. Byrd gave in. Above all, he wanted to get to the North Pole.

The first job was to find a base for their planes. They decided on Etah, in Greenland. Greenland is a very large island, northeast of North America.

The men went by ship to Etah. They had a hard time getting the planes off the ship. The water was full of floating ice cakes. The beach was full of rocks.

Not a tree grew in this cold, bare land. The men had to build a runway for the planes out of old boxes. The Eskimos helped. They had never seen a plane before.

Byrd talked over his plans with his mechanic, Floyd Bennett. "There will be many dangers on a flight to the Pole," Byrd warned him. "We might crash or freeze to death. Will you go with me?"

"Of course!" said the tall young man with the bright blue eyes.

Byrd and Bennett flew west of Greenland to Ellesmere Island. This was nearer to the Pole. They hoped to make a camp there.

They flew over rows of mountains. Ice and snow covered everything.

When he got back to Etah, Byrd spoke to the other men. "I shall never *order* you to fly over Ellesmere," he said. "You must decide for yourselves. Who will come?"

Every man stepped forward.

They finally found a landing place on Ellesmere. They brought in gasoline and oil. They brought guns and camping outfits. There were skis on their planes so they could land in the snow. It took fourteen days of hard work to get the new camp made.

Then they started exploring, flying north. They saw miles of land no other man had ever seen before. They saw frozen lakes. They saw beautiful deep valleys. But it was very dangerous flying among the high mountains.

More snow came. It was very cold. The oil for the planes froze. The men's fingers froze, but they worked on. They hoped to find a way over the mountains to the Pole. Now they knew why it had taken Peary a lifetime.

The snowstorms got worse and worse. Winter was coming. MacMillan said it was too dangerous to make any more flights. He gave orders to return home.

The planes were taken apart. Byrd was sad. He was sure he could have reached the Pole if he had had more time.

He said to Bennett, "I shall fly to the Pole next year. And I want you. Will you come?"

Bennett's blue eyes blazed. "Of course!" he said again.

Byrd said, "*I know that the airplane will conquer the Arctic. And the Antarctic as well. It will be dangerous. It will be difficult. But it will be done—soon.*"

Chapter **6**

North Pole Flight

Bennett looked at the newspaper stories. Everyone, it seemed, was trying to get to the Pole. The famous Norwegian explorer, Amundsen, was planning to go by dirigible. A dirigible is a balloon-like airship. The French and the Russians were trying too.

"We'd better get a move on," Bennett told Byrd.

Byrd said calmly, "Don't worry. We'll be there!"

Friends thought Byrd was being reckless. His father said, "I'm afraid you will never come back."

Mrs. Byrd smiled to herself. She remembered the boy who had gone around the world alone.

Byrd said, *"Somebody has to explore. It's the job I picked for myself. And I'll come back."*

He knew he would have to fly over sixteen hundred miles of polar ice. So he planned carefully. He studied oils and engines. He chose those that worked best in the cold. He bought fine boots and furs. He ordered special foods for the icy weather. He bought the best instruments to help him in his flight.

He found 50 men to go with him, a good plane, and a strong ship.

It was beautiful in the Land of the Midnight Sun. But Byrd had endless troubles. Each time he tried to get his plane off the ground something happened. One day the plane's skis were broken.

A young Norwegian flier, Bernt Balchen, came to help fix the skis. He and Byrd became good friends.

"Put wax on the runners," Balchen said.

Byrd did so. He had a runway built from the top of a hill to the water. Men smoothed out the snow.

The test flight was good. A little after midnight on May 9, 1926, Bennett said quietly, "Ready!"

He and Byrd got into their flying suits. The motors warmed up. A man cut the holding ropes with an ax. The plane sprang forward and headed up into the northern skies.

Byrd and Bennett took turns at the wheel. They watched the seas of ice glittering under the midnight sun, the strips of cold gray water. Would they make it to the Pole?

Suddenly Byrd saw a leak from the oil tank. The oil covered the window. *"The motor is going to stop,"* Bennett wrote on a note to Byrd. *"We'd better make a landing."*

But there was no place to make a landing. They must keep going!

Byrd dropped one of his instruments. It broke as it hit the plane's floor.

Now he had to figure where they were by "dead reckoning," without any instruments.

Nine o'clock . . . then 9:03. Byrd tapped Bennett on the back. *"The Pole!"* he shouted. His voice was tense.

Bennett shook his head to get the noise of the motors out of his ears. *"The Pole!"* A big smile lit his face. They had made it!

Chapter 7

Through Fog to France

Five hundred small boats greeted Byrd and his crew in New York harbor. Streets were jammed with people who wanted to see him. He went home to Virginia for a visit. His brother Harry, now Governor of the state, welcomed him. It was a happy time.

President Coolidge made Byrd a Commander in the Navy. The National Geographic Society awarded him the Hubbard Gold Medal for his flight.

He accepted it, saying, *"Admiral Peary was the first man to reach the Pole by dog sledge. I believe he will be the last. The dog sledge must give way to aircraft. The United States must plant its flag at the South Pole. It has never been there or anywhere near it."*

Byrd had already asked Bennett if he would go with him to the South Pole. But first Byrd wanted to fly across the Atlantic. He wanted to fly in a big plane to show that people could travel that way. He was sure planes would carry passengers and cargo across the country and across the ocean.

Many people were against the flight. They thought it foolish. But Byrd had something to prove.

He bought a plane with three motors.

When he tried it out it turned over. Byrd's arm was broken. Bennett was so badly hurt that he could not go on the flight. This was a dreadful disappointment to him.

In his place Byrd got Bernt Balchen, his Norwegian friend. He asked Bert Acosta and Lieutenant Noville to go too. They were well-known fliers.

While Byrd was planning his trip, Charles Lindbergh flew to Paris. He flew alone in a single-engine plane. Others tried too. But Byrd would not go until everything was right. He laid his plans with care, as he always did. He wanted this trip to be a success.

"The worst thing that could happen," Byrd said, *"would be not to reach Paris."*

Before they left, the government made the plane a United States Post Office. Letters were carried aboard. If they reached Europe, it would be the first transatlantic airmail.

Slowly the great plane *America* lifted into the air. Balchen shouted for joy.

Soon Byrd wrote in his diary, *"Raining, fog, clouds low."* They had to run their engines at full speed to get above the fog. That took more gasoline than they wanted to use. They tried to fly higher, hoping to get strong winds to carry them on.

Hour after hour the fog continued. Night came. Now there was fog and darkness together. Each man took his turn at the wheel while the others slept or kept watch.

The fog was so thick they radioed ships to tell them where they were. The ships radioed back.

"I reckon we're over Paris at last," Byrd said, the following night. "But it's too dark and foggy to land." His voice was full of disappointment.

Later Byrd saw the flash of a lighthouse below. They were near the sea. Byrd wanted to get to Paris. All America hoped he would. But he had his men's lives to think of. He must come down before they ran out of gas.

There was no landing field. They must come down on the water. "Stand by to land!" he ordered. There was a crash. The water sliced off the landing gear and the wheels. Something hit Byrd a sharp blow above his heart.

The plane began to fill with water. The men got out and swam around in the dark. They climbed on a wing of the plane but the wing sank.

Lieutenant Noville managed to pull their rubber boat from the plane. He pumped it up. The mail was in a waterproof bag. They put it in the boat and rowed ashore.

They walked wearily along a dark road to a village.

"Where are we?" Byrd asked.

"You are at Ver-sur-Mer. Welcome!"

They were in France! Later they went to Paris. They were cheered everywhere. The French people loved these brave young fliers. The Americans had flown the first mail across the Atlantic!

Chapter *8*

Over the South Pole

Commander Byrd stood on deck as his ship headed south. It was 1928. He was off to the Antarctic at last!

Byrd was thrilled, yet sad too. He would be away from his family for two years. His four little children would hardly remember him when he came back.

Would he come back? Brave men before him had explored the Antarctic. Some of them had not returned.

But Byrd had planned his trip for months. He had chosen 82 men to go with him. There were newspaper men, radio men and photographers. There were scientists, mechanics and sled-dog trainers. There was even a nineteen-year-old Boy Scout, Paul Siple. He was the envy of Boy Scouts everywhere.

Best of all, there was Byrd's friend Bernt Balchen. Byrd turned to Balchen now. "I wish Floyd could have shared this adventure with us," he said. Floyd Bennett had died.

After several months, they finally reached Antarctica. Byrd looked about with excitement. There was only ice and snow as far as the eye could see. Great mountains rose in the distance. Byrd hoped to fly over them to the Pole.

Two other groups of explorers had reached the Pole by foot. Byrd hoped to reach it by plane.

First they must build a settlement. "We will call it Little America," Byrd told the men.

It was very cold, but the men worked long and hard. They unloaded the ships. They built some bunkhouses and supply houses. They built a radio shack. They built tunnels under the snow to connect the different houses. They had to hurry to finish before the winter storms.

Winter in Antarctica is bleak and dark. There is "night" for four long months. The men spent the time indoors. They saw only the same faces, the same small rooms. The Sunday movie was a big treat.

The men had jobs to help pass the time. They studied. They made plans for spring trips. They sent out weather reports. Often it was 60 below zero!

Paul Siple's job was collecting penguin skins for scientists back in the United States. Byrd also asked him to collect live penguins when the weather got warmer.

When the time came, Paul found the job harder than he had imagined.

"Watch!" he told Byrd one day. The "black-coated" birds were gathered in one corner of their pit.

As Paul and Byrd watched, the birds made a ladder of their bodies. Some birds hopped on the backs of others. Still more climbed on their backs, and so on.

"They look like circus acrobats!" Byrd laughed.

Soon the ladder of penguins was higher than the pit. Then the penguin at the top jumped out onto the snow outside.

"They've been doing that every day!" Paul said. "We have to keep catching them and putting them back."

"I'm glad you're keeping busy," Byrd teased.

In November it was spring and everyone was busy. Small groups of explorers started out with dog sleds. Some would study the weather. Others would study the land. They would hunt for minerals in the ground. When had the rocks been formed? When had the land frozen? Had animals ever roamed here?

The more men could learn about the Antarctic, the more they would know about the history of the earth.

The mechanics worked on the big plane, the *Floyd Bennett*. On the afternoon of November 28, 1929, it was ready to try to fly to the South Pole.

As the plane rose into the air, Byrd gave a sigh of relief. They had made a fine start. He felt sure they would succeed.

Bernt Balchen was at the wheel. "I feel wonderful," he grinned.

Harold June, the radio operator, smiled back. "Me too!"

The photographer, Captain McKinley, started taking pictures. He would map the land between Little America and the South Pole.

At eight o'clock they flew over a group of their own explorers. The men looked like little black bugs. They waved. Soon they were lost to sight.

Byrd was the navigator. He planned the route. But little was known about the country. He had to make decisions as they flew.

Which was the best way between the huge mountains? The sun shone so brightly on their snowy peaks that they seemed on fire. It was hard to see.

Finally they started through a pass in the mountains. But the plane was too heavy. It could not lift high enough to get above it.

"Quick!" Balchen ordered. "Drop something overboard!"

Which should it be, gasoline or food?

Byrd made up his mind quickly. Food. They dropped a 125 pound bag overboard. The plane lifted!

Then the wind pushed them down again. "Quick! More food!"

The plane rose with a sudden jump. McKinley was busy taking pictures all the while. Byrd was busy with his maps and instruments, reckoning where to go. Balchen was steering.

Now they were flying above a great plateau, a high level land of ice and snow. It stretched for miles and miles in all directions.

Balchen saw clouds gathering. Should they turn back? It would be impossible to fly back through the pass in a storm.

They kept on. They were so close to the Pole now.

At 1:14 in the morning, Byrd said, "I figure we're at the Pole!" His voice was filled with quiet excitement.

"Fly beyond it a few miles," he told Balchen. "Then turn to come back."

Just before the turn, Byrd opened the trap door. He threw out a small American flag. The flag was weighted with a stone from Floyd Bennett's grave. Bennett had been with Byrd on the North Pole flight.

Now Byrd had been to both Poles. He and his men were the first to fly over them. At last the American flag was where he had said it should be. It was a proud moment for Byrd and for America.

Chapter 9

Alone

Honors were heaped on Byrd. The United States made him an Admiral.

He wrote a book about life at Little America. And he got ready for another trip. "Antarctica is still the unknown continent," he said. "There is so much to find out. We must go back."

Paul Siple went with him again. Paul was older now. He was put in charge of the dog teams.

Byrd wanted to build a small base as close to the Pole as possible. "The winds of the world are formed near the South Pole," Byrd said. "If we can chart these winds, it will help weathermen everywhere."

Byrd knew that life at the far base would be hard and lonely. He felt he could not ask anyone else to live there. So he decided to live at the base alone for six months.

His men hauled supplies and food over the snow by tractor. Near the mountains they dug a pit in the snow. They sank a little shack in it. It was only nine by thirteen feet. They set up machines for studying the wind and weather. They set up a radio tower.

The fierce winter was almost there.

It was time to say good-by. Byrd shook hands with his men.

"See you in the spring!" Byrd said. He tried to sound cheerful. But no one could smile.

The last sound of the tractors died away. Now there was only silence and whiteness everywhere, thousands and thousands of miles of it.

Byrd was busy each day. There were so many things he had to do. He must keep the fires going and cook his food. He must take the weather readings and make out his charts. He wrote down what happened each day in his diary.

"...Today I had to dig the pancakes out of the pan with a chisel. . . . Freezing my hands, nose and cheeks, I mount the pole to the wind vane."

70

The dark winter months passed slowly. Every day Byrd spoke on the radio to the men at Little America.

Then Byrd fell ill. The fumes from his kerosene stove poisoned him. He did not want to eat. *"But I force myself to eat,"* he wrote.

The radio broke down. He had to crank it by hand to make it go. It took all his strength. Sometimes he tried to climb the ladder that led out of doors, only to fall back. Sometimes he slept for hours on end and woke up cold and miserable.

The snow drifted mountain high. There were many storms. They sounded like thunder around the shack. The cold fell to 74 degrees below zero. It was hard to breathe.

The radio men often did not get answers to their calls. They worried about Byrd. They felt sure he was sick.

Byrd tried to say that everything was all right. He did not want them to risk coming to get him. "Just the same," Dr. Poulter said, "we're going to get him." Dr. Poulter was the second in command.

He chose two other men. They set out with tractors to reach Byrd. Twice they had to turn back.

Byrd knew they were trying a third time. He used all his strength to climb the ladder. He lit kerosene flares to guide the tractors. When he saw nothing on the miles of snow his heart fell. He did not know if he could last much longer.

At last he saw a searchlight moving in the distance. The men were coming! "In a little while," he thought, "I will see friends and hear voices talking."

Byrd stood straight. But he did not dare walk to meet the tractors. When they came up, he said feebly, *"Hello, fellows. Come on below. I have a bowl of hot soup waiting for you."*

Then he fell down into the shack. The men were shocked to find how thin and weak he was.

It was two months before he was strong enough to leave the shack. The men stayed with him now. Perhaps he had made a mistake to live there alone. But he had found out many things about wind and weather. His records were complete. He was proud of them.

Chapter *10*

New Discoveries

Byrd went back to the Antarctic three more times!

He went once before World War II, then twice again after his wartime duty.

Each time Byrd and his men made new discoveries. They discovered new islands, mountain ranges, glaciers and plateaus. They found a strange area completely free of snow. They made an air map of most of the coastline of Antarctica.

They studied the weather and the rocks. They tested new instruments. They tried out new ways of living in cold weather.

"Some day," Byrd said, "men may live on this continent. Minerals are in the earth. The sea is full of life."

In between trips Byrd gave lectures. He wrote books to tell people about the strange lands he knew so well.

In 1955 Paul Siple went to the Antarctic with Byrd again. He flew with him to the South Pole. On the way they had lunch. Byrd looked at the large tray on Paul's lap.

"I remember when we had chicken sandwiches and a thermos of coffee," he said. "And we had to be careful that those didn't weigh too much!"

"And now we're having hot pork chops and fried potatoes," smiled Paul. "And we're being waited on!"

Byrd's eyes had a faraway look. "I remember the open planes and the cold winds that blew through them."

"And now," Paul went on, "huge planes carry mail and cargo and passengers to all parts of the world. Everything that you've dreamed of has come to pass. Hasn't it, sir?"

Byrd smiled. "Not everything. But we have made progress."

He turned to Paul and spoke earnestly. "There is still so much to learn and do. There will always be adventure for those who dare. You're one of them, Paul."

Byrd's life was full of adventure up to the very end. He died in March, 1957.

Byrd had done what he wanted to do. He had explored far places and added to people's knowledge of their world. Best of all, he had found that men can endure hardship and come through with high hearts.